A QUIET AFTERNOON

NEESHANT SRIVASTAVA

Made with ♥ on the Notion Press Platform
www.notionpress.com

For the man that tries too hard but his efforts bear no fruit.

Contents

Contents

Contents

Preface

'A Quiet Afternoon' has been published before. It speaks of my trials and tough times in my life. This is the landscape of life where nothing is revealed so easily. I am always reminded by my parents, elderly and especially my mother that a human life is very precious and we must try to make the best of it. I never understood her words and often thought that a brown skinned man like me that did not possess a beauty that people could find engaging was never worth anything. But as they often say,

"*The road is long,*

With many winding turns,

That leads us to where,

Who knows where..." from a popular song,

and suddenly after years of darkness and the desire to burn and burn like in a fire, I shed something that had hindered me for ages. I don't know from where things started making sense like I had unravelled the mystery of life. A wise man is the ultimate loser, I feel, and the person that has nonthing worthy to speak of and acts rather innocently, like the greatest fool, finds the greatest truth in life, unawares. It's like the Mother Nature around us. A mountain takes ages to form and after it does, it stands high and a nonsensical man cannot even gauge its magnificence and beauty. It stands like a king with a majestic crown. Thus we humans must learn from nature. Do not be in a hurry to discover things and find out what's hidden. Let life dawn on you instead of reaching out for it. Patience is a great virtue and the lack of it can make you digress from your path and that is what usually happens in this world. No wonder the world is in the dark in spite of the great progress of the human race.

PREFACE

These set of poems attempt to help someone on the path. We must lend a helping hand to others if we can. Don't always secure your burning fire, spare a thought for others too.

1. A QUIET AFTERNOON

Our journey begins at eighteen,
Not knowing that time will gradually pass,
That we will not be young for good,
Some people start even before eighteen,
But this life has to be lived to the finish,
There are nearly thirty years for us to develop,
For we shall begin to get the fruit of our actions,
By the time we reach fifty,
Did we develop into a well-rounded, balanced person,
Have we evolved into a human that has a heart,
Do we feel the pain of others,
Have we risen above petty beliefs of race and colour,
Have we risen above the animal in us,
Are thoughts bothering us still, away from peace,
Do we live in a constant air of regrets,
Can we sit quietly in the afternoon and breathe,
Are we tossed constantly in a trampoline of negativity,
Have we really been successful in our own eyes,
Are we at peace with God,
Have we done what He expected us to do,
Have we just lived for ourselves,
Don't turn away O! Human,

Don't turn your eyes away from life,
Don't deny that we become what we do in life,
Pray if you have missed the road,
The end is not too far away,
Get ready to do better the next time,
God was never our enemy.

2. AN END TO 'I'

This world is hooked on the 'I',
The soul sings a song,
It is the song of God,
The 'I' so huge denies the message,
It cannot bend at all, it's too heavy,
The past million lives are clinging to the 'I',
Things that have been done and forgotten,
The 'I' has taken a definite pattern within,
No one has the energy or the will to break it,
As children we are assured to be the very best,
This forms a peaceful connection with the past lives,
Those that are deprived of self-respect, berated and belittled,
Do summarize later in life as abuse,
Can someone bend before criticism and deprivation,
And count themselves as someone that needs self-improvement,
Can we try to change ourselves rather than our environment,
The boastful 'I' will not allow us to move even an inch,
How can then we hear the voice of the soul,
Which is urging us to do the same,
To give up all that we are made of,
To take the ultimate test of love,
To die right now and not hold a grudge,
The 'I' grows stronger with time,
It assumes thick and dark blankets of ego around itself,

The end to 'I' is farther away than we imagine,
This game has become bigger than God imagined,
And He cannot by magic throw some light on the street,
Each one must rise by natural processes,
Each passing human is obliged to himself and others,
To break the 'I' leaving a blessed land of souls.

3. DOES ANYONE LOVE SEAN

God asked the father,
Do you love Sean,
God asked the mother,
Do you love Sean,
What can you do for him,
What have you done for him,
He is sick and dying,
Replied Pat's father,
I love Pat more than myself,
I have spent sleepless nights beside him,
When he carried a slight temperature,
I have my eyes pinned on the troubled child,
Just to save him from his disasters,
That boy should not die, give him some lifesaving food,
When Pat went without food for a stretch,
I quit my life for my dear Pat,
I never bothered for my mornings or evenings,
Mother of Pat loved him even more,
Something that even Pat did not know,
She saved him from the hands of a witch, his wife,
When he got married as someone plotted his end,
Pat has the most wonderful life he could imagine,

He has turned into a saint,
He is a free man, thanks to the love of his parents,
Where are Sean's parents when he needs them,
They have left him here to die,
Does anyone here know what love is,
Has anyone been ever loved in their lives,
Well, of it's not true, then it is not love,
Father does not love his children,
Mother has no love for her children,
If that is false then where do they go,
When the child needs them,
What will they do for the child.

4. IT DOESN'T HAPPEN

A dull and sweet man walking the road,
And reaching the very end,
Someone doing different from what he is told,
And not carrying a feeling of enslavement,
A little crack within for the light to seep in,
The 'I' bowing down before the soul,
In spite of carrying past load same as others,
It has never happened in the history of time,
Some stranger actually walking the path of truth,
Being true is like the sound of death,
For the soul is insane and shall push you to hell,
Humans with the courage to act as humans,
And not some mundane breed of cattle,
Someone through cracks of insanity,
To become the sanest alive,
To engender the perfect and magical brain,
A balance rarely found in history,
A dull flower becomes a stunning beauty,
Under the beautiful gold light of the sun,
Hell, actually becomes heaven,
Endless meadows of delight with a silver sheen,
The sweet prod of the beaks of timid birds,
To produce a beautiful interruption,
In oceans of silence,

Let's play the game again,
And live to see the glories of heaven.

5. JUNK HAS LEFT ME

There I sat with host of thoughts,
I had been hurt, and that's not new,
I sat in deep analysis of the intruders,
Comparing them with me and feeling good,
Of course, I am better off than them,
But the analysis went deep into the night,
When my window turned from bright to dark,
I am sweating and restless, the conclusions were useless,
Why, I have done this all my life,
My brain like a worn-out machine, is heated up,
It cannot do the manipulations any more,
My life meant to pick follies in others,
Where am I going, please,
I think I will join the meditation class,
Perhaps that will cool down the machine,
And leave me with blank spaces of time,
Maybe I am an under achiever,
I have done nothing to take note of,
Well, I don't spoon up in any conversation I know of,
They say you find peace when you reach the moon,
I suppose I did something recently,
It just blows my mind off,
Something like walking on the Mars,
And the junk has left me, I think,

I am no longer interested in other's biography,
To find time that just belongs to me,
I am trying to dig out thoughts from an obstinate mind,
You have tortured me enough, haven't you,
Dear God give me some thoughts to play with, I beg,
But the train has subsided,
It has been docked somewhere forever,
Pass me some coffee, I am all for it.

6. LIFE SONG

I have been an addict,
Wondering what use this life is,
Even if it were to end abruptly,
Many years went by until I realized,
That life is a song,
That must be sung to its entirety,
A song that never even began has no meaning,
For the song erupts from pain,
A song comes from our struggles and strife,
Reflecting the purity of the soul,
A pure soul can change someone completely,
And show him the path to success,
To sing a complete song that even benefits others,
But how do we change ourselves and decipher our song,
No father, no mother, no brother, no sister, no God,
Can change someone or bring about reform,
And I have known that addiction is the worst kind of bondage,
When we slacken our principles and draw curtains too soon,
For another life will not be given so soon,
There are those that live a hundred,
Never knowing that life indeed is song,
Too scared to be slashed by a blade,
Too scared of the heat of an ordeal,
Too prejudiced of the innate pain inflicted,

By human forces and higher power,
For some the song has almost ended,
A beautiful rendition of an angel song,
God is smiling with the book of song in his hands,
That boldly gives glimpses of a beautiful soul.

7. NICE WEATHER

There's a calmness in the air,
The weather is nice,
The intense heat and then the rains,
We were unhappy then and are unhappy now,
Nobody has uttered a word since morning,
People go about doing their work,
Wash and clean and fill up the water jugs,
The past never existed,
People have forgotten what they said or did,
Someone in a car knocked a two-wheeler couple dead,
But raced his car to safety as if nothing happened,
A man cannot understand why his son has a deadly disease,
A handsome man in his fifties is so unsettled in his mind,
His face does not reveal his discomfort,
Why is he so irritated and a volcano of negativity,
The great disorder and storm within,
Have been pushed under the rug,
And it's a nice weather with the clouds and rain,
A great respite from the heat,
People with piles of regrets,
Will go far to correct their lives,
But to begin is to undo a clump of wool,
That needs too much time and patience,
And when the bell rings, they become too rigid,

One has to then live with it till the end,
The young have nothing to worry about,
They do not have clogged minds,
They can enjoy the season and many more to follow,
Their gaiety gives us assurance,
That indeed it's a nice weather,
There is great peace in the world,
And the heat has finally left us.

8. NOTHING CHANGES

Children of eighteen set off on a journey,
Wondering what life is all about,
Expecting some unusual and exciting things,
To become an adult is their greatest dream,
And not be treated like prep school kids,
Desire of heavy things like wife, job, kids,
They can't wait to join the huge family,
Years unfold drop by drop,
As they capture the beauty of life and youth,
Money in pockets and those lavish buffets,
And then a strange happening common for all,
Next thirty years almost amount to nothing,
Their hair begins to turn grey and children move out,
There are no changes in them,
The same old hunger for instant pleasure,
The same old desire to line up for good food,
They have been globe-trotting all these years,
Hoping the new air could bring big changes in them,
But when they are back home,
The same old suffering and irritation over small things,
The same old anger and craving for this and that,
The passing years did not do anything at all,
As we were all expecting a new person to emerge,
It is the same old story like it has been,

The river always flows in a set pattern,
So many people have come and gone,
Nobody disturbed the rhythm or shook obstinate walls,
Nobody changed at all.

9. RICH MAN'S RIDDLE

From the wombs of time emerges the rich man,
He's got ships, yachts, and mysterious palaces,
There's no doubt in him that being rich leads to happiness,
His mind works feverishly for ways to multiply his money,
His bank account adds zeros with every season,
Until he goes from poor to the richest around,
His house becomes a go down of objects,
Most of them sound rather unfamiliar,
There is a crowd of people waiting at the door,
For just a glimpse of him and maybe for some help,
It is better to have excess than to be deficient,
When money decides the quality of one's life,
He's immersed in buying acres and acres of land,
He's just turning from rich to filthy rich,
He's the talk of all women that have their eyes on the rich,
He has everything but the food does not go down too well,
He has everything but time,
He has everything but cannot get sleep at night,
He has abundant but others seem to be enjoying it, not him,
His eyes have dark circles and no hair left on the head,
His eyes cannot see more than his worries,
Of having control on the wealth accumulated,
And of expanding it even further,
There's not enough money, he feels,

No one likes to look at his ugly face,
But the women don't mind,
They just want to have a good time,
The rich man is running too fast to his grave,
One day someone might steal everything he has,
He is prone to a nervous breakdown, a panic attack,
He is thinking of ending the drama,
With a shining gun in his drawer loaded with three,
He is searching for silence and peace of mind,
He wants to be alone and leave all that he holds,
He wants to run away to the quiet hills, perhaps,
The rich man's riddle will repeat itself time and again,
There's no escape when you lack abundance,
And when you have it, the riddle presents itself,
And then there's no way out.

10. THE STING

Life means a set of incessant problems,
They don't seem to cease until we lie on the pyre,
Call anyone, any age, they can feel the sting,
God made a part of each life, abnormal,
It's hard not to think and focus on the sting,
It can destroy evenings and give scary dreams,
That feel like too exaggerated in the deep night,
God's words are like the cycle of a tree,
They don't seem to push their growth too much,
One has to be patient like the sage settled on a rock,
While his long white beard becomes a shroud of satin,
The sting will pass as its path is too far away from good,
God just wants to hear about our own actions,
He just wants us to do what is right,
For we alone then would be packed and sent,
In that empty omnibus far away from here,
The sting causing agent will burn in hell,
God then severely questions our belief in the process,
Do we have the courage to do our own act,
Far away from the organized factory of the human race,
The sting shall melt if God enters our being,
As we become the voice of our soul,
Yet it happens once in countless years,
Just like a shooting star across the sky,

Overpowering the sting will not give us peace,
As there is a hidden sting in its womb, to explode,
Sometimes its best to silently suffer the pain,
For nothing shall last forever.

11. THIRTY IN VAIN

Every man and woman have thirty years,
To accomplish a life of desire,
It's stringent at the top but supple below,
Paint on the canvas of creation your will,
And you shall see the colours emerge,
As you cover the long journey of your choice,
Some have become the creator of great empires,
Where meagre men walk under the colossus,
Don't regret being poor living on fist of grain,
You shall never walk those streets of dull and dreary,
Your car like a two-room luxurious apartment,
It's got tiny lights within and room for champagne,
Someone walked a different road in thirty steps,
An endless, rough, sacrificial, and lobsided journey,
To the zenith of a human being,
To meet a new person with universal soul,
That man vanished into thin air after countless debacles,
His past will not push him to let everyone know him,
Or carry a universal vendetta of avenging his poverty,
What is a man with all his belongings,
It shall stay to spark controversies and duress,
After the colossus is gone carrying nothing with him,
Thirty steps are all we own,
Stand up and take action right now,

Or else the world would be rife with new faces,
All seeking life and the stars.

12. THREE ROCKS

The two most ruthless and cruel people,
They left their son to die,
Father landed in the most defamed city of the world,
Leaving behind a land of ease and comfort,
Leaving behind an easy life of endless parties,
All for the sake of his children,
How can someone be so cruel and heartless,
Filth and dirt written all over the city and its people,
Nobody in the world can imagine a life in that city,
How can a mother leave her son crying,
When the child did outrageous acts to hurt him,
Maybe the city weather had taken its toll,
Father beat the boys and used bad language,
But each time the child was almost dead,
They revived him with all their strength,
When the lad was young and wed the wrong girl,
Mother stood like a pillar to free her son,
True love comes from the most ruthless people,
Those that are too soft on the outside are enemies,
The boy learnt a great lesson of love,
He loved his parents in spite of their cruelty,
He loved all that he happened to meet,
And all played games in trying to destroy him,
The city hard as a rock with stretches of waste land,

Piled with sewage from overflowing gutters,
The smell was just too much to bear,
The boy spent a big part of his life on broken roads,
The trees were swelling with dust and grime,
Almost thirty years and the city changed,
Hell had turned into heaven,
The air with fragrance and young leaves dancing in the wind,
Three rocks with a love that was true,
The lad had entered bliss,
Sometimes we don't understand love,
The people that are cruel, ruthless think about you, always,
Their words are a hammer to make a shape out of you,
Keep their word, listen to them, love them,
Remember you have just one life.

13. TODAY IS THE DAY

Today's the day it shall be decided,
Either my life will change,
Or I shall be captive of my room for a year,
Another exam of my life awaits judgement,
I seem to have failed in most exams,
I could never find some work at all,
Like a monk, a sanyasi, living on alms,
Living on the kindness of other people,
Why am I someone of another planet,
Like a destitute, a handicap on crutches,
Why can't life happen to me as well,
I am a byproduct of the city I live in,
They do not offer a job to suit my skills,
As if I had many skills or any skill at all,
God made a perfect cocoon for me,
I lived with my mother some time ago,
But she's gone and I am left all alone,
Today is D-day,
It will decide if I fly away,
Or crawl on the ground for good,
And I already know the result,
Like a bird with torn wings,
Crashes into the waters of the sea,
Destiny was not made for people like us,

We just stare in the silence for some motion,
Thank you, God, for failing me again,
I just know that you have a bigger plan for me,
But when will I actually see the plan unfold,
I am afraid, I may not live very long from today,
Sometimes I feel I cannot reach You,
Yes, I am worthy of another year,
Sitting in silence and digging into books,
I just should not give up.

14. YOUNG YOU ARE

This is the age to hammer,
To blow fully and completely,
At a wave that's ever changing,
On the heartbeat of life,
To take pain and hurt,
To go the wrong way and more,
To dive into the deep abyss,
To challenge the norms as we know,
To hurt the body and mind,
And take the plunge to disaster,
This is the time to sow,
The seeds of life and move forward,
To go the wrong way,
But never be swallowed by it,
To touch the cliff but never fall,
To walk on disaster but listen,
To the guiding voices around us,
For they have seen,
What we are yet to see,
Young you are,
Please don't shut your eyes and follow,
Like it's safe and sound,
To walk the known road,
Time shall wait to open,

The doors for you,
That shall set you free.

15. YOU A LEAF

You are just a leaf in the universe,
Your whispers may not reach the skies,
You are so timid and frail,
Your decision to follow the moon,
And not the sun,
Makes you an unheard romantic,
Don't just blindly follow your heart,
You will crumble before you crumble,
Do not deny what you already know,
That the world is disease and violent storm,
Do not trust the leaves around you,
Their glossy green is just a facade,
They will take away the sun from you,
And leave you to die,
Do not try the road of death,
You may not survive to see that day,
That some great ones have seen,
You are just too weak and average,
Nothing much is expected of you,
You a leaf cannot carry the world,
On your nothing shoulders,
The creator is not even looking at you,
Come let us die together,
We have always amounted to nothing.

16. WHY DON'T PEOPLE

Why are most evil,
Why don't people be good,
For if it goes bad it really goes too bad,
People throw stones at good,
They make them feel like evil,
While we still feel we are good,
Nobody from the skies tells us so,
More the good, worse the life,
As if we are constantly walking on fire,
No one can bare the sight of the good,
They'll try to put you off track,
Until you fall and follow their ways,
They want to take your life,
They'll force you to end your life,
Thus, each one of us decides to be evil,
For evil means instant glory and abundance,
Good takes an eternity to bear fruit,
Only Christ could bear the cross,
And not be cross with his crucifiers,
We are too ordinary and weak,
We work by creating fear than being fearful,
There is no one among us,

That can walk forever carrying,
The load of goodness,
But one day the fireworks shall end,
And we have to answer some questions.

17. WHAT ARE YOU LOVE

It's a silent day today,
There's no sign of any breeze,
The leaves on the trees hang lifeless,
My mind occupied by matters on hand,
Matters that will make me sad somehow,
My loved ones silenced and gone,
The walls of my room stare at me silently,
They have no news to give me,
Or utter some words of disapproval,
Of someone cross with me for no fault of mine,
I watch the hours flow into noon,
I am ready to begin the next part of day,
Somewhere deep in the horizon,
There is a subtle movement,
Looks like a baby breeze is shining through,
It enters my open window after shaking some leaves,
It touches my forehead and something flashes,
I feel love for someone that I knew,
It vanishes just as soon as it came,
I try to hold that moment and smile,
Is that what love truly is,
A feeling of complete bliss,

It comes and touches and leaves,
When I am not even with the one that I love,
They have long gone away,
And I thought I knew love completely.

18. THIS IS HOME

My youth sang with the Ganges,
A child in a hundred minds,
Knows not where to go or headed,
I am wandering in deep dark nights,
When the earth stands still with shut eyes,
Mother sounds inhospitable and barren,
I hear no sound in the dead leaves,
This child has to leave for better weather,
Where the girls turn out in every nook,
And this smoke and drink to lose senses,
Life is better in cubicles and lecherous nights,
Let me lie low, free from those gloomy street lights,
Eleven years and something pulled me back,
Like a fool I walked into my home,
This place is alive and dazzling like New York,
Something in me is born, a poet,
And I am born, like this stillness and peace,
This place abandoned long ago,
Like a dumping ground of all filth,
All its children left long ago,
While I circled my old school for ten more years,
This is serious and sad,
As the children find hope,
In dazzling America too pure,

I hear voices of silence,
As this sweet place breaks into a song,
Cuddling me like a baby,
I have enough for company,
I love home for allowing me,
To melt into this moment right here.

19. THE LAST PAGE

The last page is real,
The evil will be reborn,
That man that's gone was selfish,
The passer by is just not aware,
That moments separate him from complete silence,
The good is seen as some moments,
That the goer seemed to have just stumbled on,
The father is a complete villain to children,
He hardly did anything for them,
The holy man rejoices,
That he arrived at his last page,
In this mean and unsparing world,
Where the dirty mind speaks and rules,
Years spent as altruistic condensed to a moment,
Which the world could never see,
It's time to rest and enjoy a different world,
Fully in tune with nature's rhythm,
One that comes must go,
Perhaps a heart remotely,
Could feel the heart of the going,
Perhaps he saw the soul of the holy,
There could not be a greater man,
Who never sang of himself when alive,
And tossed his life for others,

Perhaps the going man saw the higher,
Who was mighty glad with this son,
The last page wants to show more of,
A man known to just a few.

20. THE HEAT

All the people have left it cold,
For we all have a fire within,
We must let it burn into a flame,
Go to the source if you can,
That is your greatest teacher,
Follow him till the very end,
He has been especially sent,
To kindle the fire of your soul,
Don't let your own mind come in your way,
When you follow your guru,
You don't calculate or think ahead,
You just dive in to the water,
And follow his wishes,
Remember it is a long journey,
And the guru may not be with you,
Till the very end,
And that you may falter at a later stage,
He will demolish you completely,
When the 'I' within you is destroyed,
And you emerge a new self,
Meeting the real person in you,
Bow before the heat, my friend,
It is not an impossible task,
Millions before have done it,

But they all sought guidance,
In each one's life a guide has been given,
We need to recognize our guru,
Let's all get together,
And reach the very end.

21. THANK THOSE

Thank those that gave you this life,
That gave you a place in this world,
That gave you eyes to roam the depth of beauty,
That holds us spell bound,
That gave you words for you to express,
That burnt their world to kindle yours,
That lit the fire within you,
That you may feel the person within,
That gave up the life of king and queen,
For the sake of the children,
That put an end to their own life,
And live for just you and only you,
That stood as pillars when fear surrounded you,
That gave you a chance to be touched,
By the gracious hands of the Almighty,
That sang the song of goodness and nobility,
So that you may find your way,
How they resolved to save a soul,
And lend you the eternal life in heaven,
Thank those that did not want a pebble in return,
No mansions, no gold, no motor, no money,
Only just as we may be safe and sound,
That we may find the truth,
Just as they did find out,

Thank those that did not blow the trumpet,
Of their effort to save you,
Suffering insults sometimes from their children,
Always remember they were always,
One step ahead of you,
Let's thank them forever.

22. SEASON OF SPARKLE

This is the season of sparkle,
There are lights and happy sounds to hear,
The cloud of laughter has burst on us,
Are you happy by stealing it from someone,
Drowning the other one in sadness,
Have you cheated someone,
Hiding your crime by sugar coated talk,
This light then will not last long,
One day you will submerge in darkness,
All the laughter and gaiety will vanish,
For a man must repent for his crimes,
In this life and many to follow,
This is a silent time disaster,
Time decides what fate shall come,
To those that have wronged,
And made someone else suffer,
With their greed and evil intentions,
Don't revel over other's blood,
It's not them but God,
That shall punish you,
See all the sparkling lights have died,
While you are soaked in the heat of sorrow,
Destiny is nothing but a fruit of our actions,
It butchers those that revel,

After taking away life from someone,
There shall be no sparkle ever again,

23. RIVER OF GRIEF

There is a river of grief,
It strengthens with age,
It flows with force,
Some jump off after a short ride,
Some go against the flow,
And reach where they wished,
Only after getting off the river,
See those people on the banks,
Leaving very few on the river,
Very few will raise their hands,
And let the river take them,
Such are insane and foolish,
Fearless and ready to face danger,
Hurt in all possible ways,
Soon they realize that the river is endless,
They are far from those on land,
That have carved out a dream,
Got what they desired and more,
But for that fleeting thought of uneasiness,
That seem to surface frequently,
The one on the river has reached the end,
They lie safe on land bruised, exhausted,
They have managed to cross the mighty river,
To meet the maker in His kingdom,

Everything is bright and cheerful,
The river of grief was too long for one life.

24. LISTEN TO THE SAGE

The sage sat alone in the forest,
One man walked up to him,
Asked O Holy! Why are we here,
I have done it all in one life,
I have been a son, husband, father,
When I was young, I wanted a woman,
When I got one, I wanted children,
When I had children, I wanted a promotion,
I wanted to amass everything material,
I became the richest man in the city,
I was always surrounded by people,
Many among them were strangers,
I hosted parties and drank late into the night,
I have also had secret relationships,
Not known to my wife or children,
I have tasted everything there is to taste,
Years ran away too fast in fun,
And now there is this loneliness,
My children are not with me anymore,
I have failed to know of any purpose,
Of this pleasure train called life,
You have lived your life to the full,

The sage finally opened his eyes,
And there is nothing wrong in that,
One day you shall realize the futility of it,
That day you will rise to a new sun,
And walk a road that's barren,
Where nobody ever walks,
You will find a new meaning of life,
You will not expend your energies then,
In things that lead us nowhere,
You will find you own road,
Without anyone's help or advice,
Wait for that day, my son,
It will come soon.

25. LIFE JUST ONCE

For all those that life failed,
Life is showing you something else,
Don't let life rule you,
Grasp it into you palms and turn it,
For we walk the road just once,
Bad things happen to us just once,
At the end of it lets be wiser,
By not walking the same road again,
Life has something even more beautiful,
It failed you when you were young,
It took you down the destructive road,
It ridiculed your soberness and gullibility,
It tossed you into the dungeon,
And it lasted for a million years,
You suffered in silence for,
Something that you didn't do,
You carried the load of someone else's crime,
Do not hear what the world says,
They did not come with any solace,
When you were down and weeping,
When you were in deep sorrow,
Fly away right now and don't ever come back,
Experience the earth and the skies,
You are down to the heaven song,

It's the most beautiful melody ever heard,
Don't let anyone take it away,
We live just once,
This is our time.

26. IT'S WELL KNOWN

The road to heaven is well known,
We all know what goodness leads to,
That those do that walk on fire,
That the journey is not easy,
That we have to burn in boiling oil,
To reach somewhere in life,
That the easy way is doomed,
That we are stealing our way to success,
That we have cheated many on the way,
That the outcome of it all will be terrible,
That the ghost of fear is everywhere,
That our life is an endless tackle,
Of unceasing problems,
We suffer the deluge every moment,
This never-ending train of thought,
One goes and the next appears,
Has made our lives meaningless,
Giving no time to look at life around us,
Our lives start and end nowhere,
The infamous broom is moments away,
It won't come before hell itself,
That we all must pass through in this life,
Never to be humans again,
It's well known,

There's no life without sacrifice,
The Gods did that too,
When they happened to come here.

27. FINALLY

Hundred thousand in a football stadium,
Heads rolling in waves,
Just a dump of humanity,
How many among them finally there,
Not a single in the crowd,
It is not up to us anymore,
It is not somebody's fault,
If their lives did not break into peace,
Each one of us carries our past,
Of a million births before this one,
How then can someone be free,
It's certainly going to take a million more,
Let's all do it in bits and pieces,
That's how it is supposed to be done,
A leap will be too costly,
Like walking in hell and more,
A total boycott and blame on the person,
How can someone fly while others sleep,
Allowed to go free in the end,
For no one knows what it is,
Let the world pass by, my friend,
Let mornings come and evenings go,
Let people and their carnival,
Let the music play late into night,

While people have a dance together,
The crooked man has finally made it.

28. DELICATE AND GONE

It's the narrowest of all paths,
Manly and you stand to lose,
Womanly and you are a lost bird,
One touch more somewhere on the road,
And it is broken beyond repair,
It is so long that it seems impossible,
It requires a phase of death,
When the outer ego shall take a beating,
It is breaking all right but too painful,
God allows you into the darkness,
And it seems to never end,
A sudden brightness somewhere,
Does not mean its end,
That's why it is rightly called,
The end of all roads there is,
Delicate it is you cannot say you're there,
Stay away from manly touch if you can,
Until the bugle sounds,
And it's the end of everything,
We cannot take it easy and drift,
We have done that too many times,
This is our time and we must get it right,

No matter what,

Or else be entangled in blues forever.

29. BLACK CLOUDS

Black clouds hovered over the boy,
His attempts at life ended in disaster,
They said why didn't you wish,
When you were a child and soft,
Why did nobody ask you,
What you wanted to be, then,
You little one worth nothing at all,
Look at those eyes that have dreams,
There is something they want to do in life,
Right from a tender age,
Looks like your ship never had direction,
Don't complain if now you are stranded,
In a helpless situation with no morning sun,
Your mother is running all over,
Trying to clear those dark clouds,
Not anytime soon they all agree,
Do you even have the patience,
To see it all through,
It will take an era if at all we see something,
Look your mother's now gone,
And you are all alone,
How did the dark clouds disappear,
You know longer hold string of bad omens,
The Gods have finally seen you,

Every night ends in a bright day,
Say you even have a purpose in life,
You may have even found a dream,
See you are working towards something,
You can now see the horizon clearly,
Life bows waiting for your words.

30. ACROSS THE RIVER

The question still lingers after ages,
Each one searching for a meaning,
They are all convinced with the road they are on,
Reaching an end with a mind still confused,
If this is not all then what is,
They might have seen the sparkling river,
It is the river of life,
Very few even think of going across,
Many will dive in to test the waters,
The river too deep they feel,
Right in the middle or less,
They cannot go any further,
They head back to the shore,
To the place where they started,
Very few will reach the other end,
Hearing a voice as they approach,
The other shore after ages through,
The voice gets deeper with time,
But they are still in the waters,
They have gone too deep into the river,
They are bound to make it,
Those few unafraid of drowning,
That come once in a lifetime,
Will be saved by the Almighty,

And helped across the river,
Be lost in what you do,
Do not think what lies ahead,
When you happen to search for God.

31. A SERIOUS MATTER

A letter to those that have found the easy,
If it does not hurt, then it's not worth it,
What are all these people up to,
Harm the meek till they are destroyed,
Sin by night and planning by day,
You long dumped your folks in the graveyard,
If it means something to you,
Being human doesn't come quite often,
In fact, it comes never at all,
You got one and wasted it,
You play your music late into the afternoon,
But children you have reached the sunset of your life,
You cannot set right what wrong you did,
Time is running out,
For those young ones still have a chance,
And will let it go waste,
That is the cry of all humanity today,
It is a serious matter,
It took us too long to get here,
How can we just let it go,
Almighty is out with His torchlight,
He is trying to reach us,
We just have to walk straight,
And close our eyes when in pain,

For that too shall pass,
And we head to a bright tomorrow.

32. A KNOWN

People will do anything to be known,
Let them see me with wonder,
My body is my greatest treasure,
I have amassed more money,
Than all levels of consciousness together,
I never live in person on this earth,
I am always found on the celluloid,
I want to be the greatest ever on this earth,
Don't talk to me about methods,
I don't believe in principles of virtue,
I want to leave a spot after I go,
I don't believe in goodness and simplicity,
Those are the excuses of a lame man,
How can then there be a higher power,
Nobody ever found a way to get there,
I am the only one in this world,
Look how I float in this world,
Come down O! soaring kite,
There's a slender string that holds you,
Why you are quite an unknown,
The trees don't know you,
The walls of your mansion don't know you,
Those flowers in your garden have never met you,
Those seeking some of you have been refused,

Those that know you, know you for a while,
And then the world turns with new faces,
You don't know yourself on your death bed,
Or the one reflected in the mirror,
Even the cold currency is a stranger.

33. BUDDHA PURNIMA

On the day a man was born,
Only to become a saint,
To walk the road, barren and thorny,
His father never thought his son would walk,
Six years of absolute abandonment,
No one called and no one heard,
His steps in a storm of loneliness,
Where he could not hear his own steps,
Why dear Siddharth, the beautiful son,
Did you think that we don't care,
To be the one handed down in ages,
By God's divine calling,
We are looking at you now,
More eyes than before,
Show the way if you can,
We all long to go there,
These muddy roads have creamed us for too long,
We have seen the darkness for ages now,
Will God send you again soon,
What a blessed day this is,
When humanity was born again,
Now that you've come, please don't go,
As we celebrate a new beginning in our lives.

34. A DREAM

Lately I have dreamt a dream,
Like a young lad hoping for big,
Don't look back if you can,
For there lie deserts of failure,
Like God purposely made me fail,
Like it may come true just before my grave,
I have never seen success at all,
In these four days of existence,
The first day meant nothing,
Followed closely by the second, third, fourth,
Like I am not meant for dreams,
Like life is a river of compromise,
Like I have to take the lower anyways,
Who are then those that excel,
Are they humans like me or machines,
To extract anything, anytime, anywhere,
I want to see my dreams shattered before my eyes,
That is the reason I tried over and over again,
I don't deny the golden rule,
That the world belongs to winners,
While the rest just squirm in the dust,
And accept anything thrown at them,
And be beggars not choosers for life,
Now I see some dots of light in the evening horizon,

Some caravan seems to be approaching me in the desert sand,
I closed my eyes to the mirage,
Suddenly loud music and blinding lights hit my eyes and ears,
This is the caravan of success,
They have come to take me to the hill,
To a land of meaning,
Far away from the desert sand,
Telling me, my dreams have come true,
I am now counted among the best,
I humbly hang my head and offer gratitude,
For each one in my making,
I promise to go even higher and never look back.

35. A LITTLE HOPE

In my life I hoped the ghost to leave me,
That I would not pretend love,
That I could hear myself in the din,
That words in my ear are whispered by God,
That I do not create disgust the slightest,
That the heat would give way to rain,
The rain would give way to light weather,
That Papa and Momma would lighten up,
And Papa would play with his son again,
That time flies at times and sits still in the evening,
That the caterpillar in my box shows its colors and fly,
That the doggie grounds his head in contemplation,
That my life ends when there's nowhere to go,
That someone holds me like a human,
And loves me like the only one,
I hope to die before a sin,
For I think that I cannot face God,
I don't want forgiveness for my sins,
For I think they are one too many,
I hope I make it to hell,
For I have done worse,
I hope I can be of some help to someone,
That my father thinks I am worthy,
Let me end this life now,

I hope someone remembers me after death,
I hope it's not too difficult.

36. BOX OF POEMS

There lies in the corner a box of poems,
It carries an astounding flight,
For words are just words,
Like paper for the concoction man,
Who shall arrive with his entourage at four,
We are sunk too low if we should know,
The same words, the same legs are killing us,
The poet cannot conjure something new,
The story of the same old strife and struggle,
A man is a man and a woman is a woman,
Where can we find heaven on earth,
Singing made up jungles on the T.V.,
Life is after all strawberry flavor ice cream,
The actors smile fake to rake up piles of notes,
The box of poems is sitting in solitude,
A few words followed by deep silence,
Its cover is colored bright to invite pedestrians,
They say it's been like this for ages,
The poet buys his own books to boost sales,
He discards his own poems a million times,
Silly old thing, he remerges to make some more boxes,
A dying poet is still not dead,
Perhaps he has to learn the metric jargon,
The box is sure to bring alive an anonymous night,

Don't give up the charm of boxes of poems,
You never know who's asked you for the boxes,
It is indeed a feather in your cap.

37. DON'T WALK THAT LINE

The most foolish of all,
Has seen the road end,
Why did you want just one,
When she hasn't arrived yet,
Skimming the gold with silver hair,
How did you even carry the notion,
That this road will reach its end,
Did the God's words fall into your ears,
How can someone be so foolish and carry on,
Without no partner or off springs,
How can someone bear the slap for so long,
From this heartless and indifferent world,
They have all given up,
To the storms of the bed,
Wanting a way out of some maze,
How are you now surviving alone,
Where is the night headed to,
Does the soft and pleasant evening,
Bring hopes of something at all,
How did you bring eternity to your knees,
How did you focus on nothing,
And see the imaginary world descend,

How many Gods did you fathom on the way,
When the devils played their obvious games,
Don't ever walk that line again,
Thank the Lord you are now invisible.

38. FLESH AND BONE

What is a man in flesh and bone,
Rejected like crumbling leaves,
Carried by a fast river,
Through with life before it even began,
There's no time, what do we do,
To take a plunge is like insanity,
When there's no air to breath,
A long and arduous road to oneself,
Is too much to ask for,
We do not have the patience,
Who will make us an entity, identity,
Society has given us enough,
To make us greedy for power, money,
Like stamping the other in our glory,
Life has slipped away too soon,
When empires have been known to crumble,
And nobody can take even a grain of sand,
To their grave,
A huge gathering of people,
Circle the mundane dome,
Tossed like sand off whimsical fingers,
What is a man in flesh and bone,
Perhaps just a thought.

39. LIFE A GAME

Life is a game for many,
Very few will walk straight and honest,
Few know a game is a game unto oneself,
If we ever want to reach ourselves,
Brain pundits talk about self- esteem, confidence, worth, respect,
What have you if you are far away from yourself,
If you cannot have ears for the rumblings of the heart,
Where every sojourn is a shadow of past and a dead society,
For listen very carefully, games take you nowhere,
If caught in its web it leads to destruction and darkness,
If you follow the soul, it will take you to a land of dreams,
It will show you the peaceful land that had always existed,
Giving space to the mind leads to creative marvels,
Just like God created humans and then smiled,
This world is made up of infinite colours,
That will rarely begin to show,
If swept through life in a hurry,
Denying that there is anything in this human life,
Except being full and luxurious like a cake walk,
For once it's gone, God shall deny,
Look at the black bull carefully,
Its eyes don't squint or move,
It's not aware of its own load,
As it sinks into thick mud puddle to escape the heat,

Have you wondered, they are not even human,
God seeks us for us to plunge,
Into ourselves and follow the path,
Made with such ruthless Hands,
For there is glory on the horizon,
And He can't wait to receive us,
And if you are too deep in the game,
And cannot see anything beyond the darkness,
Don't lose hope, for life is too short,
There will be better days tomorrow.

40. LORD WILL CARRY ME

When the ride is rough and uncertain,
When my Lord seems to have disappeared,
When I'm carried by no one,
When the road seems unfamiliar,
When people pounce by shooting awkward draughts,
When I close my eyes and call within,
When the leaves present a bleak color,
When the work done so far falls short,
When disease is the voice of the season,
When I am rumored to have loved someone,
And like a fool I did destroy myself,
When I cannot stand this box of uncertainty,
When my feet cannot hold the ground,
An angel appears to remind me of the work well done,
That there is no more travel,
That the job is done and purpose accomplished,
When all I have to do is wait,
To finally leave this land to a place,
With greater promise and peace,
The good Lord will carry me,
When demons rule the air,
When the passage has become doubtful,

And they attack in harsh notes,
Trying to steal the glimpse of God,
Let the good Lord carry me,
Far away into the pinnacle of a dream.

41. PEACE IN THE HUT

See minds roaming endlessly,
Trying to catch a piece of life,
Saying I am a special being,
To which all shall bow,
In a walk amongst the crowd,
Saying I am nothing without a name,
I am nothing without pockets full,
I am too scared to cast myself in loneliness,
I must utter a word that sparkles,
I am built for others eyes,
I must harness my special gift,
And that is the only road,
I have more time than told,
Till I find peace in the hut,
Why is the world run by a handful,
I am taller than all of them,
A tribute to my genes and forefathers,
There was no one ever like me,
Life is simple if thought over,
There are no bumps or holes,
No roadblocks just the shine,
I am the greatest that ever was,
Living in eternal peace,
Until Gods call me again.

42. PLEASE LISTEN

Please listen to the age-old voice,
It is pushing you towards a known mark,
It is making you secure,
Against hurt, pain and wanderlust,
It is giving you food on your table,
It is giving you comfort, love and hope,
It is giving you good health and your own children,
It is clear on how you should live,
The voice is clear and wants your safety,
It wants to give you a stable mind,
It wants to give you a good life, and recognition,
It suggests on how to exploit your talents,
Do not listen to those gypsies and hobos,
They could never a life out of their own,
We shall quietly walk to our graves,
After giving our children a wonderful life and thought,
So that they too follow our footsteps,
Who said that life is hard and mysterious,
Problems can never be bigger than ourselves,
With an astute mind there's nothing that is impossible,
We shall find our way out of the mess,
Our minds are those of a genius,
Just use it and find a solution to any problem,
Life is fun and it has always been that way,

Don't forcibly make yourself sick and stricken,
For that road only leads to destruction,
Let's travel the world and enjoy life,
Please listen, time is running out.

43. SHORT PLAY

Life is a short play,
We continue from where we left off,
There is this possibility that lingers,
For each man and woman,
Of reaching the very last bend,
Of going beyond the 'human',
Please do not waste your time,
In useless chitter- chatter,
Don't be lost in words and their weight,
Act now in silence and with purpose,
For it is possible, absolutely possible,
God has given you an ambience to flourish,
Don't deny and leave your road,
Don't change with the seasons,
Looking for the perfect oasis,
He wants you to aspire,
For the divine light,
His arms are raised to receive you,
At the other shore,
Alas you could feel Him and hear Him,
It's strange how each of us has the perfect realm,
To live and grow, accepting our challenges,
Let this be your last cup of tea,
Get ready to fly to paradise,

And also feel the paradise we live in,
Let's not waste a single moment,
The time has arrived to end this merry-go-round,
For it's a short play,
And we are gone in a moment.

44. THE LAST CHANCE

You have just one,
You are walking into a crowd,
Among many lost travelers,
On the pinnacle of the street,
They do not know where they are headed,
Like corpses strolling in a graveyard,
It is mighty easy to be lost and gone,
On the busiest highway,
Where everyone rides,
There in no time to think,
Or even consider some other alternative,
Before you know, you have come too far,
The only thing left to do is to keep going,
And see the final stop sign,
It was an opportunity given to you,
Before you realized that it was indeed one,
Shatter and smatter are the only things real,
Life had totally lost any form,
Days are just a stutter and waste,
Nothing seems to have come out of life,
Convinced that you were always right,
The road you walked was the only road,
That sage was in fact the devil,
What he utters on his long beard is unreal,

He was always pondering on useless things,
His world is just made up,
God is too kind you know,
This can never be the last chance.

45. THE STORM

The storm came in too many times,
A heart wrenching story of too many failures,
Each time a thought of what is not meant for me,
There must be something that I ace,
A trend soon established of falling off the cliff,
As if I actually reached the cliff,
I pushed my art with a lot of love,
As they say love never goes wrong,
It is most untrue I admit over and over again,
For what is love in today's world,
Why is God so adamant to destroy my effort,
And still expect me to rise and shine,
And carry on with the failure forever,
How can decades not suffice for constant failures,
Well, I don't want anyone to read my lines anymore,
But what good am I without the very thing I failed in,
The lull after the storm suggests carrying on in futility,
But I am not the master in my trade,
For I haven't seen success after failure,
In fact, I have never seen any success,
There is a time for everything they say,
For now, I must dig into my art some more,
For my life depends on it,
It makes me fluffy like a wet flower,

Let the storms take their toll,
This time I am not turning back.

46. THE WHEEL'S SPINNING

Look around and find frightened eyes,
Don't talk about the subtleties and goodness of life,
We are far ahead buried deep in reality,
We long for a feather in our caps,
And it's not sparing the young and just arrived,
The wheel's spinning,
Video generation is flooded with ideas,
On how to make a quick buck and be free,
It will perhaps lend us a fearless life,
Look at the extreme weather conditions,
Each city has a big storm in its womb,
And it threatens to destroy humanity,
Fear is the only word that sells,
Fasten your seat belts and prepare for a rainy day,
Make more money for a little is not enough,
Humans as humans do not matter,
We are all but numbers in a jail,
The news is flashing day in and day out,
The end is coming nearer and nearer,
Disaster is imminent and no one will be spared,
The time may differ but the blade shall fall,
There's no time for a picnic, songs and poetry,

We must rush to our cubicles,
For there's a hammer that will fall,
And spell a sudden death,
What did we do so wrong to see this bend,
There's no time to reason,
Money and more money are the only cure,
Each one with the horror of death,
And the place we go to after the end,
But the wheel's been spinning,
Like it has for ages,
Albeit this time it's harder,
And no one will be spared.

47. NEON CITY

You are sure to lose yourself in neon city,
One step in and there's no way out,
The loud city and the dazzling neon,
The distractions to enslave the mind,
To bouts of limitless pleasures,
After a hard-fought cubicle battle,
The night's already been planned out,
For men and women who know not,
What the wild dissipation means,
It's the neon city and there's not room for sadness,
The old folks have been aptly sorted out,
The world is young just like it always was,
Catch the highway if you do not know,
Where you are headed,
It's the world of the weirdos,
In a cloudy smoke room and neon blitz,
Let's pass the bug around and taste life,
It's a soft road towards liberation,
Neon city is a point of no return,
Look all the folks are joining in,
From all over the world,
The neon city is too crowded,
A dense smog of hell to set you free,
The party's too loud and everyone's excited,

The mind has ceased to the blinding neon,
And it goes on and on.

48. WHERE ARE YOU

The world travelled west,
While I travelled east,
I never knew that I had a thirst,
Of finding You,
I stood still in the tense air,
There were the usual sounds and words,
I walked I don't know where,
This world a collage of great men and women,
All spectacular in just their existence,
I am not one of them and never will be,
I just happened to finish my assignment for the day,
I am headed home for lunch and sleep,
I am a little off in my performance,
And the bosses keep yelling at me,
I have left all hopes of You,
You were meant for those collaged greats,
And people who were better equipped,
In looks, knowledge, courage and holy verses,
Do I have a question on my mind,
There's nobody that can even attempt to answer,
The whole eternity is dumb and indifferent,
I didn't come here to make a mark,
Or to find You somewhere,
What can I make of the remainder of my life,

Knowing that extreme sacrifice is what God sees,
Celibacy is something that I detest,
I was never pure enough for that penance,
Pile of sin is just too high,
Who am I then to come near You.

49. WHERE ART THOU TALENT

A great artist has seen poverty,
The way no one has,
They are all crowding around him,
Wanting to finish the silent beauty,
Mozart never played his music,
Graham Bell never budged in science,
Albert Einstein did not create the unthinkable,
Julius Caesar was never born,
Alexander never drew a never-ending line,
Impoverished and deserted these men were crucified,
The world could never figure out their genius,
Each one determined to blow them to dust,
But God lived in each one of them,
And no one could touch their work,
As each one got his right place in this world,
For when you walk alone, you walk alone,
You'll never find a lone shoulder to help you across,
There will be violent storms to rubbish your mettle,
Stand stronger right now, time is calling,
Do not envisage sweetness and kind words,
They make a dull and insipid soul,
A challenge is meant for brave men,

Stand now and go beyond,
Those peaceful shores await you.

50. WHERE'S HOME

Young at eighteen and no one has answers,
Whom do you ask and what do you do,
The older seem to know, offer certificates,
That one's too slow, low self-esteem, no confidence,
Only a miracle can save you my son,
Yes, the young at eighteen is faced with problems,
He looks at those messages in the brain,
The people know exactly what to do and pass it on,
What the young does is of no value,
Neither those people care nor anyone else,
To try something outrageous, parents have got it covered,
They shall berate and deny and even kick the worthless,
Out of the house so that he leaves for good,
Knowing well that the poor baby will return,
When the hunger beats hard on him,
Where does the young go,
He's reluctant for the unheard,
And does not like people giving commands,
Maybe he then decides to leave home when time comes,
And to never return to his abusive parents,
Then life is fun with freedom,
Stay out late and spend his own money,
The era of questions long gone,
When he becomes a star at the evening bash,

A strange question came to me today,
When my fifty year old self asked a question,
Where's home.

51. THE ROAD

We are on our own chosen road,
Will we reach the very end,
With tail that's too long for comfort,
With a kiss of promise to never end,
There is relief on the right and the left,
Fun n' games and a light show,
Enough to dazzle our eyes and stop for a while,
A billion options and we are to select one,
There is a thin road that does not exist,
To focus on nothing cannot be an option,
We think the darkness has ended when it has not,
We anoint ourselves as spiritual saints,
When the Buddha will not speak for months,
After he reduced to nothing,
God is generous and He loves us,
"Come again", he gently says,
Yet who has seen the sun shine ages hence,
We have a brighter chance than ever,
It takes a hair of lust to get distracted,
And we revel in a billion colors,
Pray for nothingness at death,
For the present is slipping away,
Repentance and dreams will blow us cold,
Knowing that the empire shall disappear,

Once we leave forever,
Leaving the road never walked on,
For the darkness lasted too long.

52. WHY THIS SUFFERING

Why does God give us suffering,
To suffer is to dwell in hell,
Does God actually have a heart,
How can He be so cruel,
Why Amy suffered terrible tragedies,
One shot that disfigured her mind,
She could not think and act as normal,
One shot that chopped off her one leg,
She could never walk like normal,
One shot and her inner were impaired,
She was entangled in pills,
Yet Amy survived this cruel life,
Good Amy was crucified for life,
To be good is to suffer the wrath of God,
For every good soul God has a hammer and chisel,
For He is adamant in creating a masterpiece,
He shall hammer the stone until it shines,
Like Lord Jesus in a lesson to humanity,
To suffer and suffer in silence,
Do not utter a word,
Just let the pain seep through,
And one fine day when the work is done,

He shall offer His quilt and take you away,
Far from pain and suffering.

53. YOU NEED

What do we need to survive,
Huge palaces all over the world,
That carry ornate lonely walls,
Chandeliers the size of mountains,
A huge table with a handful around it,
Expensive carpets woven by broke artists,
A huge helipad and private jets,
A huge list of helpers on demand,
Cars that do not exist for the ordinary man,
Or a small hut in oblivion,
Carrying a roof with a hole,
And when the wind blows,
The dust collects in the house,
A house with barely anything in it,
An earthen pot carrying cold water,
A bed that had cracked under the weight,
A floor made of mud,
Barely enough clothes to wear,
A small window somewhere,
With a perfect view of the morning,
As little birds feed on thrown corn,
The night like black velvet,
Sprinkled by shining yellow and white lights,
No malice, hatred, fear, anger or ego,

Eyes blessed with divine light,
That's costlier than the brightest palace,
Circle of love with no room for sadness,
Watching time pass by,
What do you need, after all.

www.ingramcontent.com/pod-product-compliance
Lightning Source LLC
LaVergne TN
LVHW091111150826
845673LV00002B/780

* 9 7 9 8 8 9 1 3 3 5 5 7 8 *